RUBANK EDUCATIONAL LIBRARY No. 37

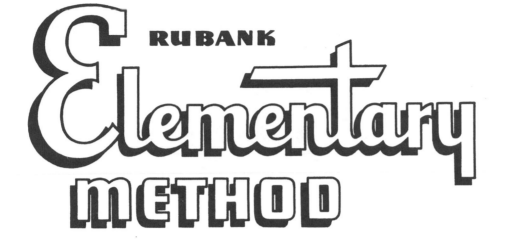

RUBANK Elementary METHOD

FRENCH HORN

E♭ ALTO or MELLOPHONE

J. E. SKORNICKA

A FUNDAMENTAL COURSE FOR INDIVIDUAL OR LIKE-INSTRUMENT CLASS INSTRUCTION

RUBANK®

HAL•LEONARD® CORPORATION
7777 W. BLUEMOUND RD. P.O. BOX 13819 MILWAUKEE, WI 53213

Fingering Chart for French Horn,
Mellophone and E♭ Alto

J. E. SKORNICKA

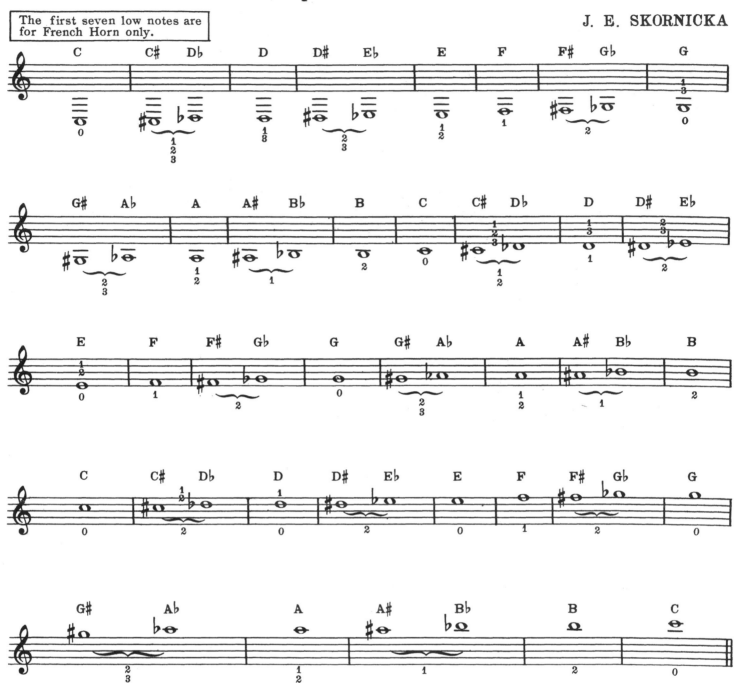

This chart contains standard fingerings, for French Horn, Mellophone and E♭ Alto. Lower fingerings for French Horn. The upper fingerings are for Mellophone and E♭ Alto. When only one fingering appears it is the same for all three.

Some of the notes may be fingered in several different ways, however this is not advisable since these fingerings may produce faulty intonation.

In some instances these fingerings are used in order to simplify difficult passages, however the intonation, when faulty, must be adjusted through careful listening and "lipping" up or down of a tone, commonly called "humoring a tone".

Rubank Elem. Meth. for French Horn

INTRODUCTION

The basic theory underlying the organization plan of this course is that good instrumental performance depends on the pupil being able to hear the desired pitch before attempting to produce it. Practically all passages in this course should therefore be sung properly as to pitch and intonation before being played on the instrument.

Correlating the voice training which the child receives in the daily singing classes with the playing of an instrument, particularly in the manner of pitch conception, should be emphasized. Pupils should be made to realize that the two processes of training are alike with the exception that the instrument is substituted for the vocal organs in the production of a tone.

To produce as beautiful a tone as possible is quite important, but to be able to play in pitch and with good intonation, should be a major objective.

Developing the ear beyond the technical performance of the pupil generally insures faster musical growth, whereas the development of tone and technic is a matter of time, during which the embouchure will develop and the ear will become more discriminating as to the quality of tone being produced.

How to Produce a Tone

1. Tone is produced by the vibration of the lips.

2. When lips vibrate slowly, the pitch of the tone will be lower than when they vibrate quickly.

3. The lips of the brass instrument player can be compared to the string of a violin. The tighter the string, the higher the tone, the looser the string the lower the tone. Pupils should be able to produce high and low tones, within a reasonable range, at the beginning of their playing careers.

4. The pupil should practice by vibrating the lips without the aid of the mouthpiece or the instrument, commonly called "buzzing." After the pupil has been able to distinguish the differences in pitch produced, by buzzing alone, the mouthpiece may then be added with the same objective in mind. As soon as a range in pitch can be recognized with the mouthpiece alone, the instrument should then be added, with the result that many of the elementary difficulties will be greatly reduced.

Where 2 sets of fingerings appear, the lower is for French Horn and the upper for Mellophone. When only one set appears, it is the same for both.

Whole Note and Whole Rest Study

First Duet

EXPLANATION OF FIRST LINE OF EACH LESSON

*)NOTE: The first line of each lesson is a review of old problems and the introduction of new ones. Each one of these lines should be thoroughly gone through before proceding with the lesson proper. The new problems should be clearly explained by the teacher, and the review problems clearly explained by the pupil. The pupil should be able to distinguish the review from the new.

Rubank Elem.Meth.for French Hn.

Half Notes and Half Rests

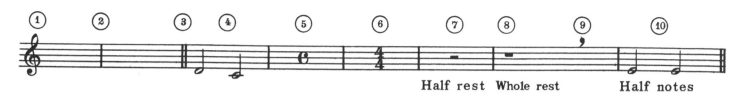

Half rest   Whole rest   Half notes

Sing before playing.

Do

Sol

Duet

Sing each line alone.   Teacher may suggest breathing places.

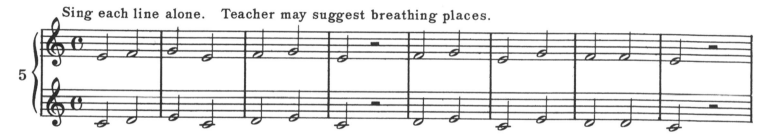

First Trio

Sol

Mi

Do

Rubank Elem. Meth. for French Hn.

Chord Building

Sing before playing.

1st Horn　　　　　　2nd Horn　　　　　3rd Horn　　　　　4th Horn

Also play each 2 measures together Result I IV I

1st　　　　　　　2nd　　　　　3rd　　　　　4th

Play same as above Result I V I

Duet

Sing before playing

Trio - In Harmony

Sharps

Melody

Counting Exercise

Duet in D Major

Rubank Elem.Meth.for French Hn.

Quarter Notes

¾ Time - Waltz

Counting Exercise

¾ Time

German Waltz

Sweet and Low

Ear Study

Rubank Elem. Meth. for French Hn.

Counting Study

German Waltz-Duet

Duet in D Major

D Major Chord

D Major Scale

Rubank Elem. Meth. for French Hn.

Flats

Melody

B♭ Major Chord

B♭ Major Scale

Duet in the Key of B♭ Major

Rubank Elem. Meth. for French Hn.

Studies in B♭ Major

Chord Study B♭ Major

Sing before playing

Folk Song

Technical Study

Quartet in B♭

f-p

Counting Study

Rhythm Studies

Counting Scale Studies

Counting Duet

If troublesome omit for Mellophones.

Low Tone Study

Rubank Elem. Meth. for French Hn.

²⁄₄ Time in G Major

Melody in ²⁄₄

Chord in G Major

Scale of G Major

Study for the Ear

Slurs

Melody in B♭ Major

Duet - When Day is Done

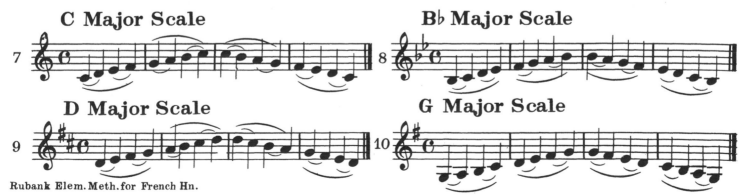

C Major Scale   **B♭ Major Scale**

D Major Scale   **G Major Scale**

Rubank Elem. Meth. for French Hn.

Eighth Notes

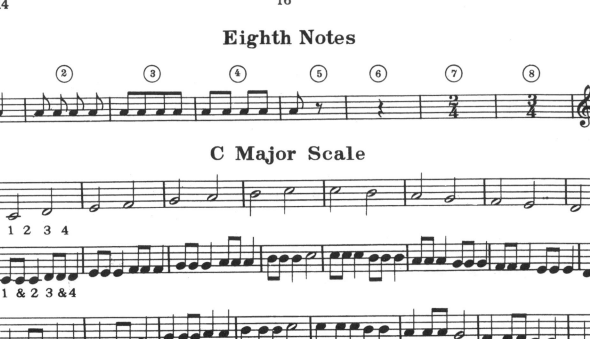

C Major Scale

Melody

$\frac{2}{4}$ Study

Two Quartets

Rubank Elem. Meth. for French Hn.

Alla Breve

Alla Breve

Melody

Alla Breve Study

Alla Breve

Melody in D Major

Melody in D Major

Alla Breve Study

Alla Breve Duet

Dotted Quarter Notes

German Folk Tume

Dotted Quarter Study

America

Dotted Quarter Study

Rubank Elem. Meth. for French Hn.

Low Note Study

Low Tone Study

Omit for Mellophone

F Major Scale

Omit for Mellophone

Mellophone - play

Long, Long Ago - High Voice

Mellophone - play

Long, Long Ago - Low Voice

Omit for Mellophone

Rubank Elem. Meth. for French Hn.

$\frac{2}{4}$ **Rhythm Studies**

Rhythm Studies

Rhythmic Study Trio

$\frac{6}{8}$ **Rhythmic Studies**

Melody

Technic Study

$\frac{6}{8}$ **Rhythms**

Rubank Elem.Meth.for French Hn.

¾ Rhythmic Studies

Waltz

Rhythmic Studies

Counting and Listening - Quartet

Sixteenth Note Studies

Sixteenth Notes Rhythmic Patterns

Sixteenth Note Study

Rubank Elem. Meth. for French Hn.

Dotted Eighth Note Studies

Loves Old Sweet Song

Farewell to Thee

Rubank Elem.Meth.for French Hn.

Rhythmic and Key Studies

Dotted Eighth Study

Maryland My Maryland

Rhythmic Studies

Rhythmic Patterns

28

Study in Tempi

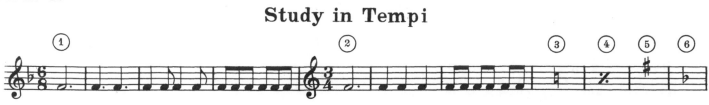

A Jig

Waltz

Folk Melody

Quartet in B♭ Major

Chord Study

Increasing the Range

F Major Chord

For Mellophone omit Exercises 1 to 6.

F Major Scale

Star-Spangled Banner

High Note Study

Chord Study

Eb Major Studies

Eb Major Chord

Eb Major Scale

Study in Eb Major

Mellophones omit No. 7 8, & 9.

Eb Major Scale

Eb Major Chord

Rubank Elem. Meth. for French Hn.

Syncopation

Syncopated Melody 2/4

Folk Tune

Study in Thirds

Rhythmic Studies

Study in Tempo

1

2

March Rhythms

3

4

5

6

A Major Key

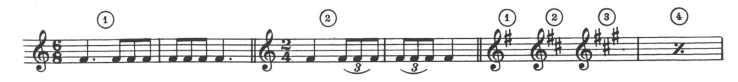

1

Triplet Study

2

3

A Major Chord

4
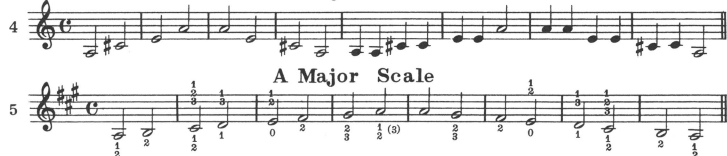

A Major Scale

5
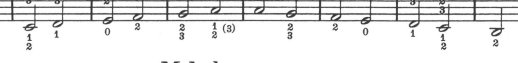

Melody

6
Also - Play ₵

7

Rubank Elem. Meth. for French Hn.

Transposition of E♭ Part on F Horn

Mellophones omit.

Upper staff given notes for E♭ Horn
Lower staff notes to be played on F Horn

Use earlier Lessons for more practice in transposition.

Ruoank Elem. Meth. for French Hn.

Chromatic Studies

Chromatic Study

Low Chromatics

Chromatic Study

Rubank Elem. Meth. for French Hn.

Chromatic Studies *(continued)*

Waltz

Chromatic Study

Mellophones omit.

Rubank Elem. Meth. for French Hn.

Examination Study
A Review of Key and Rhythmic Problems

Rubank Elem. Meth. for French Hn.

Examination Study *(continued)*

French Horns transpose to F (From E♭):

Rubank Elem. Meth. for French Hn.

Building Major Scales

The pattern for all major scales is the same. In scales there are intervals or spaces between tones which are either whole steps or half steps. A whole step will be known as 1 an a half step will be known as ½.

In major scales the ½ steps always occur between the 3rd and 4th steps (Mi-Fa) and between the 7th and 8th steps (Ti-Do)

The first 4 tones of a scale are known as the lower tetrachord and the upper 4 tones as the upper tetrachord.

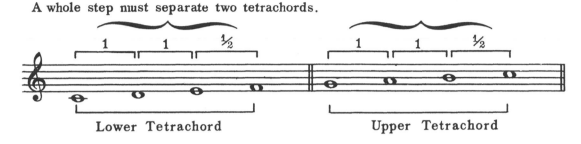

Pattern For Major Scales 1-1-½ ‖ 1-1-½

In building scales start on any tone and write out 8 sucessive tones, and than adjust, by means of sharps and flats, the tones of each tetrachord according to the major scale pattern 1-1-½ ‖ 1-1-½.

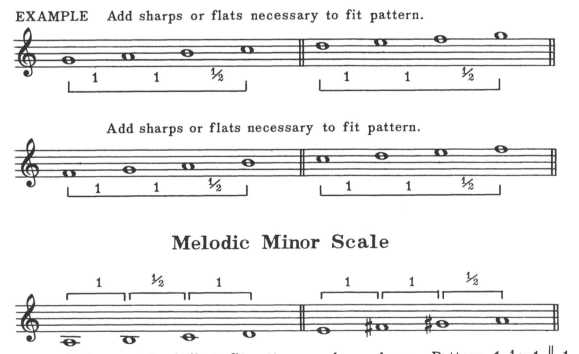

Melodic Minor Scales must be built to fit pattern as shown above.   Pattern 1 ½ 1 ‖ 1 1 ½‖
A whole step must separate two tetrachords.

Scales

FLATS

Scales

SHARPS

G Major

E Minor

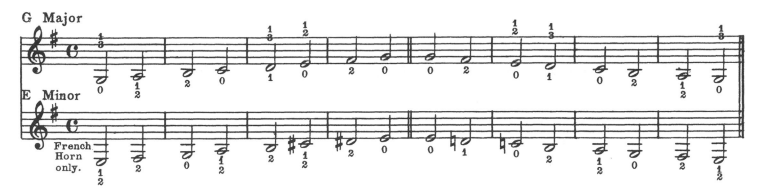

D Major

B Minor

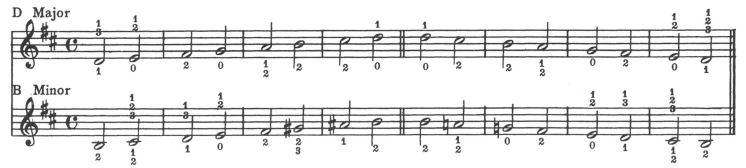

A Major

F# Minor

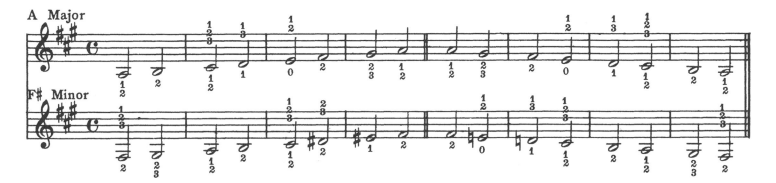

E Major

C# Minor

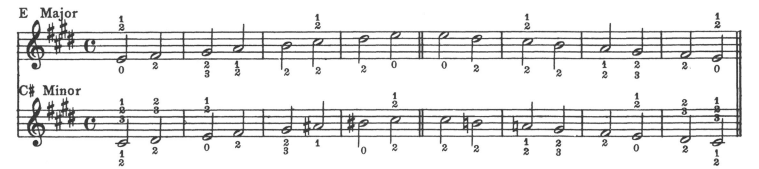

B Major

G# Minor

Nocturne From
Midsummer Night's Dream

MENDELSSOHN

From Overture
"Stradella"

FLOTOW

Swanee River

Deck The Hall

Come Thou Almighty King

Drink To Me Only With Thine Eyes

Silent Night, Holy Night
DUET

GRUBER

From Overture
"Tannhauser"

WAGNER

Duet From
Lucia Di Lammermoor

DONIZETTI

Soldiers' March

TRIO

SCHUMANN

Hymn

TRADITIONAL

Rubank Elem. Meth. for French Hn.

Song

SCHUBERT

Melody

BEETHOVEN

Rubank Elem Meth. for French Hn

Folk Song

WESTPHALIAN

From Overture
Academic

BRAHMS

Rubank Elem. Meth. for French Hn.

From
Symphony No. 1 C. Minor

BRAHMS

Allegro non troppo

Rounds